curious about

ROBLOX

BY RACHEL GRACK

AMICUS LEARNING

What are you

curious about?

Curious About is published by
Amicus Learning, an imprint of Amicus
P.O. Box 227, Mankato, MN 56002
www.amicuspublishing.us

Editor: Ana Brauer
Series Designer: Kathleen Petelinsek
Book Designer and Photo Researcher: Sara Hood

Library of Congress Cataloging-in-Publication Data
Names: Koestler-Grack, Rachel A., 1973- author.
Title: Curious about Roblox / by Rachel Grack.
Description: Mankato, MN : Amicus Learning, an imprint of Amicus, [2026] | Series: Curious about favorite brands | Includes bibliographical references and index. | Audience: Ages 6–9 | Audience: Grades 2–3 | Summary: "How do I get started on Roblox? Spark elementary readers' curiosity about the popular video game brand's history, products, and cultural impact with insightful questions and well-researched answers. Includes table of contents, glossary, further resources, and index"— Provided by publisher.
Identifiers: LCCN 2024050038 (print) | LCCN 2024050039 (ebook) | ISBN 9798892005142 (library binding) | ISBN 9798892005685 (paperback) | ISBN 9798892006224 (ebook)
Subjects: LCSH: Roblox (Video game)—Juvenile literature.
Classification: LCC GV1469.35.R594 K64 2026 (print) | LCC GV1469.35.R594 (ebook) | DDC 794.8/5—dc23/eng/20241121
LC record available at https://lccn.loc.gov/2024050038
LC ebook record available at https://lccn.loc.gov/2024050039

Photo Credits: Alamy Stock Photo/Mykhailo Polenok, 5, tom viggars, 6–7; Flickr/Pioneer Library System, 3, 18-19; Getty Images/Gabby Jones/Bloomberg, 12, Marijan Murat/picture alliance, 9; Shutterstock/Alex Photo Stock, 20–21, cfg1978, 2, 4, dennizn, 10, Diego Thomazini, cover, 1, 14–15; The Noun Project/Mohamed Salah Hajji, 22; Roblox/unknown, 2, 8, 13, 16, 17

CHAPTER ONE

When was Roblox made?

In 2006. David Baszucki and Erik Cassel created Roblox so kids could use their imaginations to play and create games. Roblox is like an online playground! Players can chat and make up rules as they play. It connects people from all over the world. It is one of the biggest gaming **brands** today.

Roblox's brand includes toys and figurines.

Roblox characters are called Robloxians.

DID YOU KNOW?
The name Roblox comes from the combination of "robot" and "blocks."

Is Roblox free?

Yes! The app is free to download. Kids under 13 should ask an adult for help. Most games are free to play. You can use a tablet or computer. Many people play on their phones. Roblox is also free on Xbox.

You can play Roblox on almost any device.

CHAPTER TWO

How do I start?

First, you must build an **avatar**. Shop in the Roblox Marketplace. There are dozens of character bodies and heads. Choose your favorite hairstyle. Add clothing and accessories. Some objects are free. Others cost Robux. You can build all sorts of looks.

DID YOU KNOW?
SuperHero is a popular Roblox character. It saves people from danger. It costs 250 Robux on the Marketplace.

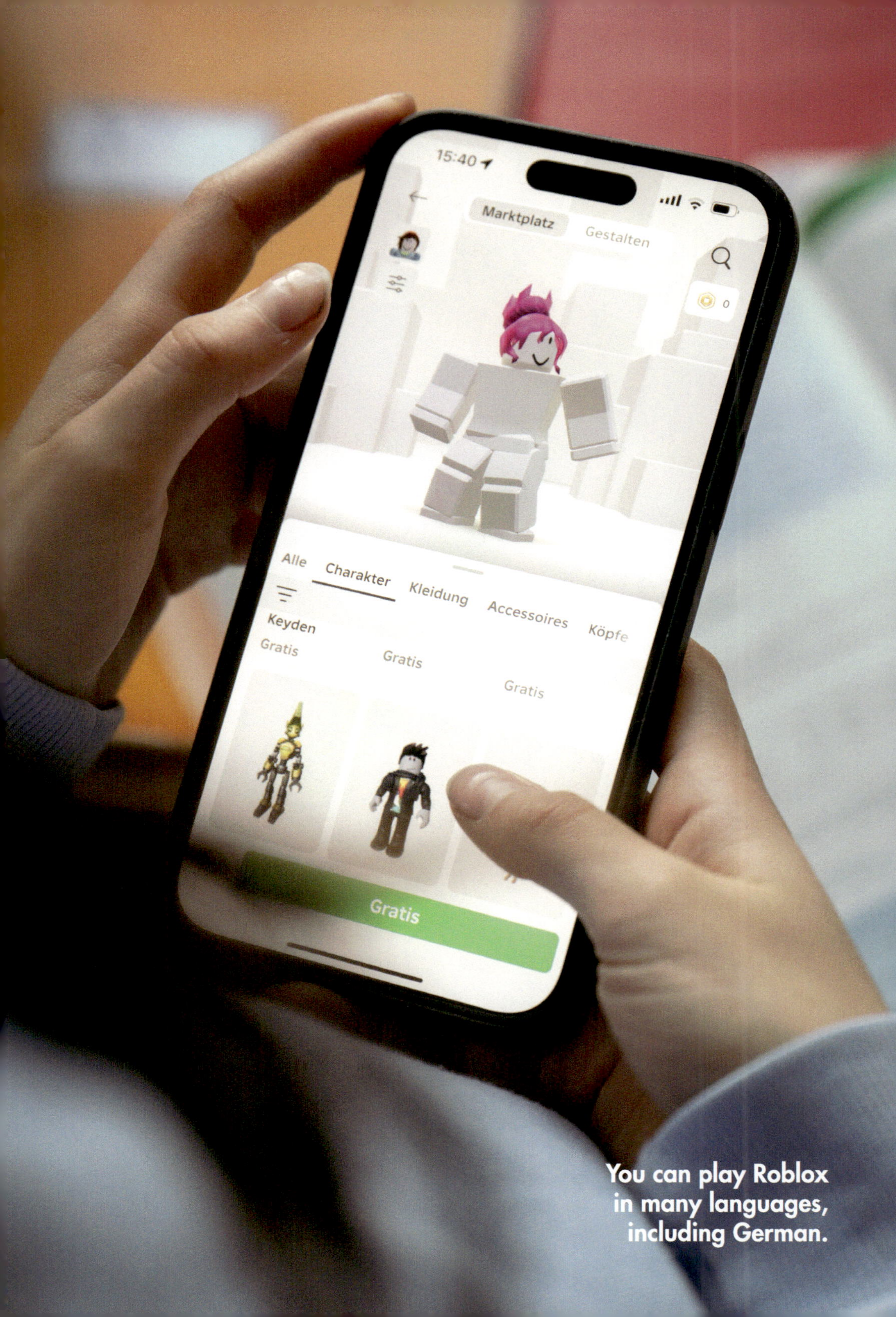

You can play Roblox in many languages, including German.

What are Robux?

Roblox gift cards are sold in many stores.

In-game money used for shopping. You can buy it through the app. Or you can use gift cards. Gift cards often include a surprise object. Get a free piece of clothing! You can also earn Robux by selling items. But you must have a paid **membership** to do this.

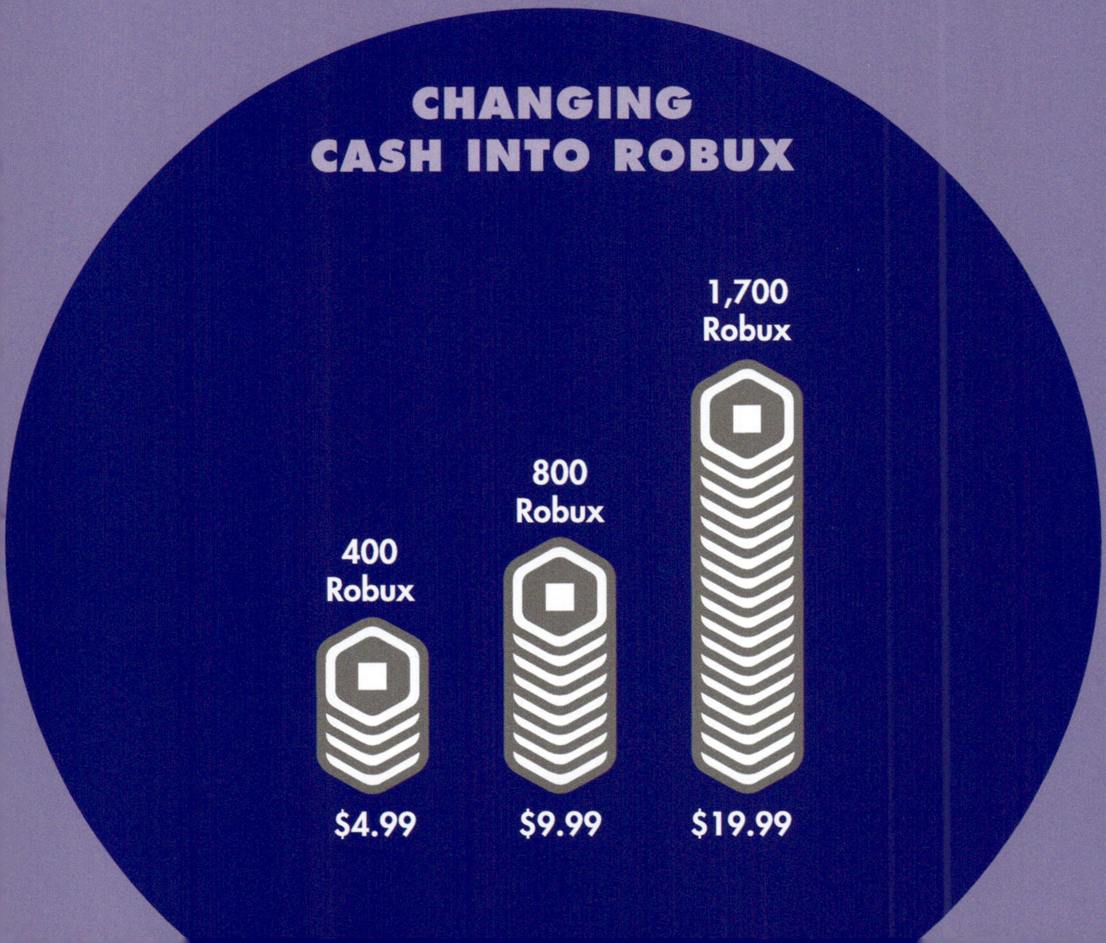

What should I play?

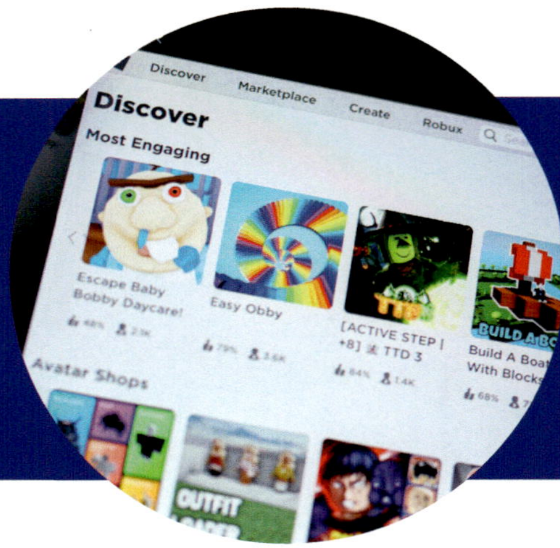

New games are made every day.

Take your pick! There are more than 40 million games in the library. Roblox games are called "experiences." There are many types. Obstacle course games are known as "obbys." **Role-play** and **tycoon** games are also popular. Find one that looks fun and join!

ADOPT ME!
ADOPT AND RAISE PETS.

JAILBREAK
BE A CRIMINAL OR THE COP. WHO WILL WIN?

BROOKHAVEN
ROLE-PLAY LIFE! OWN A HOUSE AND CAR, WORK, AND EXPLORE THE CITY.

MEGA EASY OBBY
AN OBBY GAME WITH SETTINGS FROM EASY TO HARD.

ZOMBIE TYCOON
BUILD A BUNKER TO SURVIVE ZOMBIE ATTACKS.

Is Roblox safe for kids?

Report and block someone if they are bullying you on Roblox.

Mostly. But there is danger of **scams** and bullying. Parents can choose settings to keep kids safe. They may block in-game chats or certain games. Not sure of a game? Ask an adult. Always leave the game if someone is being mean.

AGE RATINGS

ALL AGES	VERY LITTLE VIOLENCE OR UNREALISTIC BLOOD.
9+	MILD VIOLENCE OR LARGER AMOUNTS OF UNREALISTIC BLOOD.
13+	GREATER AMOUNTS OF VIOLENCE OR SOME REALISTIC BLOOD.

What are brand games?

Run your own cafe in a Hello Kitty-themed game.

Experiences made by popular companies. Explore sounds and write music on Spotify Island. Give your character a makeover in the Barbie game. Score a pair of cool kicks in Nikeland. Build a water park in Crocs World Tycoon. Or make lunch with Chipotle's Burrito Builder.

Play minigames to earn points and buy items in Crocs World Tycoon.

CHAPTER THREE

Can I make a Roblox game?

Roblox has been used in classrooms to teach coding.

DID YOU KNOW?
Many games are built by Roblox users. Alex Balfanz created *Jailbreak* as a teenager. Have you played it?

Sure! First, download Roblox Studio. It's free! It has all the building tools you need. Pick a **template** and start building your game. You will have to write some **computer code**. The app makes it easy to learn. Add parts to make the game fun or scary. Enter the metaverse!

What is the metaverse?

More than 66 million people play Roblox every day.

Are you playing Roblox? Then you are in it! This is an online world anyone can explore. Learn, play, and chat with others. Visit new places and make new friends. Try out different jobs. Master a skill or test your superpowers. Be anything you can imagine!

ASK MORE QUESTIONS

Which Roblox game is the hardest?

How do users make money on Roblox?

Try a BIG QUESTION: What type of experience would I create?

SEARCH FOR ANSWERS

Search the library catalog or the Internet.
A librarian, teacher, or parent can help you.

Using Keywords
Find the looking glass.

Keywords are the most important words in your question.

If you want to know about:

- which Roblox games are hard, type: HARDEST ROBLOX GAMES
- making money with Roblox, type: MAKE MONEY WITH ROBLOX

LEARN MORE

FIND GOOD SOURCES

Here are some good, safe sources you can use in your research.
Your librarian can help you find more.

Books

Roblox
by Mari Bolte, 2022.

Roblox
by Sara Green, 2024.

Internet Sites

Kiddle: Roblox Facts for Kids
https://kids.kiddle.co/Roblox
Kiddle is an online encyclopedia for kids.

Roblox: Hour of Code
https://create.roblox.com/docs/education/lesson-plans/story-games-lesson
Learn how to code a game by taking a Roblox lesson.

Every effort has been made to ensure that these websites are appropriate for children. However, because of the nature of the Internet, it is impossible to guarantee that these sites will remain active indefinitely or that their contents will not be altered.

SHARE AND TAKE ACTION

Try a new Roblox game.
Ask friends to join you.

Think up a Roblox game.
Write down your idea and ask friends for input.

Download Roblox Studio.
Learn how to create games and avatar items.

GLOSSARY

avatar A character in a video game.

brand A group of products owned by the same company.

computer code The instructions for a computer program.

membership Something that makes you a member of a special group; it often requires a fee.

role-play A game that allows a character to act out real-life activities.

scam An illegal way of making money, usually by tricking people into buying things they do not receive.

template Preset files that can be added to and changed as desired.

tycoon A type of Roblox game where characters build, manage, or survive.

INDEX

About the Author

Rachel Grack has been editing and writing children's books since 1999. She lives on a small ranch in southern Arizona. As a lover of stories, Disney is close to her heart. She also enjoys watching her grandchildren play Pokémon games on her Nintendo 64 console.